from MOLD to SOLD

Understanding & Overcoming Mold

From the author of
Your Home is Making You Sick
EDWARD KAMPF

WWW.SELFPUBLISHN30DAYS.COM

Published by Self Publish -N- 30 Days

Copyright 2025 Edward Kampf

All rights reserved worldwide. No part of this book may be reproduced or transmitted in any form or by any means electronic or mechanical, including photo-copying, recording or by any information storage and retrieval system without written permission from Edward Kampf.

Printed in the United States of America

ISBN: 9-798-29350-402-2

1. Nonfiction 2. House and Home 3. Cleaning, Caretaking
4. Safety 5. Cleanliness

Edward Kampf Your House is Making You Sick

Disclaimer/Warning:
This book is intended for informative purposes only. This publication is designed to provide competent and reliable information regarding the subject matter covered. The author or publisher are not engaged in rendering legal or professional advice. Laws vary from state to state and if legal, financial, or other expert assistance is needed, the services of a professional should be sought. The author and publisher disclaim any liability that is incurred from the use or application of the contents of this book.

DEDICATION

The real writer of the family, my son Zack.

The best teacher of the family, my daughter Zoe.

My mom, who keeps my book on her coffee table.

Craig Jasper who introduced and mentored me on Just Gone Systems.

Jim Greene, my fellow stinky home guy- Clean Response & Greene Air Technology.

Rob Cook, my TREC admin and friend- RealStar-U

My referral base of; Realtors, Property Managers, Community Managers, Home Inspectors, Mold Inspectors, Naturopaths, Past Clients, Eco-Solutions

CONTENTS

Introduction 1
Don't Use the "M" Word! 5
Chapter 1: Why Homes Have Become More Mold Friendly 7
Chapter 2: Ten-ish Things You Should Know About Mold 11
Chapter 3: Houston, We Have a Problem 15
Chapter 4: Interesting Mold Factoids 17
Chapter 5: Mold Inspection; Reactive or Proactive 19
Chapter 6: Common Strains of Mold 23
Chapter 7: Common Mold Inspector Methods 27
Chapter 8: Understanding the Air-O-Cell Mold Lab Report 31
Chapter 9: Remediation, Restoration, Treatment 35
Chapter 10: Intentionally or Unintentionally Failed 39
Chapter 11: Do-It-Yourself Common Mistakes 43
Chapter 12: Prep for Selling 45
Chapter 13: Water Doesn't Cause Mold 49
Chapter 14: Safe Home Remedies 51
Chapter 15: Horses & Mold 55
Chapter 16: Gluten Allergies 57
Chapter 17: Mold in the Bible 59
Chapter 18: I Need a Mold Inspection 61

Chapter 19: Mold Myths 63

Chapter 20: Purchasing a Resale 67

Chapter 21: Texas Department of Licensing and Regulation 69
- Amanda's story   72
- Allison's story- Naturopath   73

Testimonials 79

Bio...

Flyers...

INTRODUCTION

Several years ago, a prominent realtor reached out to me for a mold treatment on his million-dollar listing. The home was under contract—but it had failed a mold inspection.

When I spoke to the seller, he was stunned. His family had no mold symptoms. There had never been a water breach, high humidity, or any moisture issues. The home was immaculate.

After reviewing the inspection report, I believed the home was wrongly tested. I sent it to two trusted, licensed mold inspector colleagues. They agreed with my assessment.

But my unlicensed opinion didn't stand a chance against that of a respected, licensed inspector. To salvage the sale, the homeowner spent over $10,000 on remediation.

That moment changed everything for me. After ten years of treating mold successfully, I decided to pursue my license.

Since then, I've reviewed countless mold inspections—many of them either wrongly or even intentionally tested to fail. While writing this book, I re-inspected a $2.5 million home that had lost a potential buyer due to a bad mold inspection.

The most egregious case? A single mother saw a dirty air vent and was referred to a "trusted" mold inspector. The inspection cost $7,400. She planned to use her late father's life insurance to cover the $150,000 remediation bill. I re-tested the home—and discovered she had a mold inspector problem not a mold problem.

So why do some mold inspectors intentionally fail homes? I'd like to believe it's not intentional, but honestly—I'm very suspicious. A licensed inspector should know better.

Is mold a real health issue? Absolutely. Mold has been around since the dawn of time. FEMA places mold in the same category as other natural disasters: fires, floods, hurricanes, tornadoes, tsunamis, landslides, volcanic eruptions, earthquakes, hailstorms, blizzards, mudslides, and explosions.

Mold can also dramatically affect home value. The largest investment a person makes could become their greatest financial mistake.

But that shouldn't induce panic. Over 90% of residential mold problems require **treatment**, not **restoration**. Mold is everywhere. It's unavoidable—especially in humid parts of the country. Heck, mold even exists on the International Space Station.

As a Texas Licensed Mold Assessment Consultant, my goal with this book is to share practical, honest information—to reduce fear, avoid unnecessary restoration, and guide you through what to do if a mold concern arises.

DON'T USE THE "M" WORD!

This book was born from the countless calls I've received from anxious buyers who terminated contracts on homes they wrongly believed were dangerous due to mold.

One buyer walked away from a purchase based solely on the **outdoor spore count** in the inspection report. I didn't perform the original test, but I stepped in, clarified the findings, and helped revive the transaction. Thanks to one phone call, a family got the keys to a beautiful, healthy home.

In real estate, **"mold" is a taboo word**. People won't even say it.

- "It's just mildew!"
- "It smells a little musty."
- "It's powdery mildew."

Home inspectors avoid the term. Instead, you'll hear:

"We found suspicious microbial growth."

To be fair, only a certified lab can confirm if it's mold.

The purpose of this book is to help you understand mold—without fear mongering. Not every mold issue leads to thousands of dollars in remediation. In fact, the remediation industry doesn't want you to be educated. Their motto? **"Mold is gold."**

It's a fear-based business. And it's time to change that.

CHAPTER 1
WHY HOMES HAVE BECOME MORE MOLD FRIENDLY

Before 1980, mold remediation was rare. *So, what changed?* While homes built before 1980—and even earlier—could certainly have mold problems, awareness of mold as a serious health hazard wasn't as widespread. Mold often launched a silent attack on health, with many physicians misdiagnosing symptoms as common allergies and prescribing ineffective medications.

Older homes were typically constructed with materials like plaster, brick, and stone. While not immune to mold, these materials are less mold-friendly than modern materials like drywall. Still, if your home predates the Carter administration, your family may have faced exposure to asbestos and lead.

The creation of the Environmental Protection Agency (EPA) in 1970 signaled rising public concern about pollution. The EPA now promotes energy efficiency, but modern homebuilders often prioritize speed and cost over long-term health and ventilation.

So, what exactly changed?

- **Vinyl Windows:** Builders switched from aluminum to white vinyl windows to cut costs. Unfortunately, vinyl windows trap dust, don't drain well, and can become mold breeders. Aluminum windows had mild antimicrobial properties that helped suppress mold growth.

- **Bigger Homes, More Bathrooms:** As homes grew larger each decade, more water sources were added, especially in bathrooms—prime spots for mold development.

- **Central HVAC Systems:** Window units were replaced by centralized HVAC systems, which circulate air—and mold spores—throughout the house. Condenser coils in these systems are notorious mold breeders. Many systems are improperly sized for the home, leading to uneven temperatures and condensation.

- **Multi-Story Homes:** Heat rises, creating stagnant air pockets in upper levels. Improper air duct installation further complicates airflow and humidity control.

- **Carpet Everywhere:** Older homes often had hardwood floors, as FHA loans required long-lasting floor coverings. From the 1970s through the 1980s, wall-to-wall carpet became popular—even in bathrooms (a terrible idea). Carpet is the largest dust collector in a home, and mold thrives on dust and anything organic.

- **Wallpaper & Wood Paneling:** Mold loves paper, so wallpaper and wood paneling—especially in bathrooms—invite hidden mold growth and even structural damage.

- **Weaker Lumber:** Modern construction uses "new growth" lumber, which is harvested quickly and contains higher moisture levels, making it more vulnerable to mold than the dense "old growth" wood used in the past.

- **Bathroom Spa Features:** Jacuzzi tubs and showers with multiple heads create humidity-rich environments that are perfect for mold.

- **Tyvek House Wrap:** While Tyvek is designed to keep moisture out, it also traps moisture inside the home, reducing the home's ability to breathe and compromising indoor air quality.

- **Electromagnetic Frequencies (EMFs):** Some studies show a 1,000% increase in EMFs over the past decade. Certain molds respond to EMFs by becoming more aggressive and releasing more spores and mycotoxins.

- **Indoor Living Trends:** Today's homes feature media rooms and encourage indoor living. With social media, work-from-home jobs, homeschooling, and endless streaming, many people rarely go outside. This increased indoor time boosts exposure to any mold lurking in the home.

CHAPTER 2

TEN-ISH THINGS YOU SHOULD KNOW ABOUT MOLD

I love lists. I've got lists for everything—goals, things to avoid, even 70s rock bands not in the Rock and Roll Hall of Fame. This book includes a few lists. I call them "Top Ten," but sometimes there are 11 or 12. You've got to draw the line somewhere—this is a book, not an index.

Here are ten-ish things you should know about mold:

#1. Pay Attention to Your Health

Chronic headaches, strange allergies, rashes, brain fog, mood swings, nosebleeds, and sinus infections are all signs. If you feel better when you're away from home, your house could be the issue.

#2. You Can't Control Mold—It Exists

What you *can* control is your environment. Keep humidity low. Run ceiling fans, floor fans, air purifiers. Avoid humidifiers and dehumidifiers unless they are cleaned often. Mold thrives in stagnant air. Keep closet and pantry doors open to allow air circulation.

#3. Mold Is a Major Problem in Schools

Modern schools are sealed tight. They shut off HVAC systems on weekends and summers, allowing mold to fester. If your child has frequent after-school symptoms, mold could be the reason.

#4. Check and Fix All Leaks

Roof, attic, fridge lines, dishwashers, under sinks, drip pans, and water heaters. Re-caulk windows yearly and keep gutters clean to prevent water intrusion.

#5. Reduce Indoor Humidity

Ventilate bathrooms well—most exhaust fans are weak. Use a portable fan post-shower to allow the bathroom to reclaim normal temperature. Let your house breathe by opening windows on cool days.

#6. Clean Water Spills Quickly

Water that sits for less than 48 hours usually won't cause mold. Place drip trays under houseplants to catch spills.

#7. Clean Hard Surfaces with Water & Detergent

Don't toss items just because they have mold. Most non-porous materials can be cleaned safely with soap and water.

#8. Prevent Condensation on Cold Surfaces

Running your A/C too cold in summer (under 70°F) can create condensation, especially when hot outdoor air meets cold indoor air.

#9. Mold Grows on Everything

Carpet, wallpaper, leather, wood, shoes, belts, purses. Mold loves organic material—and 90% of household dust is exfoliated skin.

#10. Vacuum Carpet Often

The wider suggestion is to keep your home orderly. An orderly home is easier to clean. Mold inspectors have a 6th sense when entering an unkept home. If a home smells like an old book store or antique store, it's a breeding ground for mold.

#11. Keep Pet Areas Clean

Don't leave pet food or a water bowl out for long. Dogs are particularly vulnerable to mold due to weaker immune systems.

Signs of Mold Exposure in Pets:

- **Respiratory:** Coughing, sneezing, wheezing, nasal discharge
- **Gastrointestinal:** Vomiting, diarrhea, appetite loss
- **Allergic:** Itching, rashes, excessive scratching
- **Neurological:** Tremors, seizures, incoordination
- **Other:** Fatigue, weight loss, behavioral changes

Pets are family too! Let's take care of them.

CHAPTER 3
HOUSTON, WE HAVE A PROBLEM

A few years ago, a man moved from the Middle East to Houston so his wife could receive cancer treatment at MD Anderson Hospital. His realtor managed the entire home-buying process—inspectors, contractors, lenders, everything.

Six months after moving in, the homeowner discovered extensive mold throughout the home. Remediation was estimated to cost over $250,000.

He sued both the realtor and the home inspector. The judge awarded him $650,000 in damages.

The inspector, certain of his work, sent his report to reputable colleagues for review. They confirmed it was thorough and nothing was overlooked. So, he countersued.

During the second trial, it came to light that the homeowner had shipped his furniture in a non-temperature-controlled cargo container from the Middle East. The furniture sat on the open sea for two months, soaking up humidity.

The judge reversed the original decision. Case closed.

I've provided depositions in similar cases, explaining how mold can develop in homes and apartments. In this case, the outcome could've been very different had a mold inspection been conducted during the purchase process.

Many luxury real estate agents are requesting mold inspections as a standard part of every home purchase for their clients.

Again, licensed mold inspectors take on that responsibility and help protect all parties involved in a real estate transaction.

Whether home buyers are shipping furniture from overseas, using a cross-country moving company, or just loading up a U-Haul, it's vital to understand mold—its causes, effects, and impact on health.

CHAPTER 4

INTERESTING MOLD FACTOIDS

Mold comes in many colors—white, blue, red, green, and black—depending on what it's feeding on.

Mold is a fungus, but fungi include much more than just mold. They also include mushrooms, yeasts, rusts, puffballs, smuts, truffles, and morels.

Here are some fascinating facts you might not know about mold:

- **Tiny but Mighty:** Approximately 250,000 mold spores can fit on the tip of a pin. By the time you can actually *see* mold, it's already colonized into billions.

- **Mold Has Three Modes:**

    1. **Dormant** – Comfortable and inactive.

    2. **Offense** – Actively growing when moisture or humidity is present.

    3. **Defense** – Sporulates (releases spores) when threatened.

I once treated a home and re-tested it the same day. Oddly, the spore count went up after treatment. Curious, I tested again the next morning—spot clean. Turns out, mold panics when attacked. Like the defenders at the Alamo, it fought back fiercely. No need to discuss how that ended.

- **Mold Can Revive:** Dead mold isn't always truly dead. Unless it's *denatured*—meaning its cellular structure is destroyed—it can come back when conditions allow. Mold spores have a protective cell wall which is the outer protective membrane. It protects the protein against environmental stresses.

- **Denaturing Is Key:** Most store-bought mold sprays don't denature spores. They claim to kill mold, but most don't.

- **Kilz:** Great for covering stains before painting, but it doesn't destroy mold.

CHAPTER 5

MOLD INSPECTION: REACTIVE OR PROACTIVE

Many home sellers avoid pre-listing mold inspections out of fear—fear of jeopardizing the sale or uncovering costly problems. *"Why go looking for trouble?"* they think.

I get it. As both an inspector and remediator, I understand the concern. But if there is an issue, it's better for the homeowner to take control before a buyer discovers it. The alternative? Losing a potential buyer.

Some buyers have had prior mold nightmares or have family members with compromised immune systems. A clean mold report can offer peace of mind and comfort.

The Mold Inspection Process

Inspections often start *after* a residential home inspector flags "suspected microbial growth." That's the reactive approach.

A thorough inspection begins with **fact-finding**:

- What are the concerns?
- Any health symptoms among the occupants?
- What's the home's history?

We're not doctors, but we're trained to recognize mold-related symptoms. We seek a **hypothesis**, not a diagnosis.

The Visual Inspection

We start at the top—literally. Is the roof in good shape? Water intrusion starts there. Then we move to:

- **Attic:** HVAC system, drip pans, plenum, ductwork
- **Home inspection report:** Areas flagged for water damage or microbial growth

Modern home inspection reports have expanded from 30 pages to over 100. With thermal cameras and moisture meters, inspectors catch more—but also defer more.

That's where we come in. If there is a mold suspicion, we are the ones to assess it.

Common Red Flags We Check For:

- Indoor humidity above 60%
- Moisture content over 17%
- Dirty or moldy air vents
- Disconnected dryer vents
- Moldy return air intake

Inspection Tools and Techniques

- **Moisture Meters:** Help detect mold risks in walls and floors
- **Thermal Cameras:** Identify hidden leaks and moisture pockets
- **Visual Checks:** For discoloration, water intrusion, and structural damage in all accessible areas. (We do not go on top or under a home). We search for potential water penetration or signs of current or previous issues. This allows the mold inspector to locate where moisture is entering to determine the source of the issue.

A comprehensive visual inspection can be very quick, depending on the size of the property.

We inspect:

- Under sinks
- Dishwashers
- Behind fridges
- Laundry areas
- Garages

Sampling Methods

- **Air Sampling:** Uses cassettes with a glass slide to trap spores for lab analysis. We compare indoor samples to an outdoor "baseline." Indoor spore counts should be lower than outdoor levels in a healthy home.
- **Surface Sampling:** Uses swabs or tape to analyze visible growth.

Remember: Mold isn't visible until it colonizes. Spores may still be present even when you can't see them. That's why proper testing is essential.

CHAPTER 6
COMMON STRAINS OF MOLD

"**I** have black mold in my home!!!"

It's usually the first thing homeowners tell us. And while I never scoff at mold concerns, every mold inspector has heard this panic more times than they can count.

The culprit people fear is *Stachybotrys*, often called "black mold." *Black Mold* is its colloquial name. Ironically, it's more dark-green and slimy than truly black—and you can't identify it just by sight.

Understanding Stachybotrys

Stachybotrys is dangerous. It produces **mycotoxins** when disturbed, which can lead to serious health problems. It grows on damp materials rich in cellulose—like sheetrock that's been wet for a long time.

Symptoms may include:

- Nasal irritation
- Migraines
- Brain fog
- Chest tightness
- Respiratory issues
- Skin rashes
- Fatigue
- Even death in extreme cases

It's often found in homes that have sat vacant, flooded, or had long-standing leaks. It rarely just "shows up" on an air vent. In clean, well-maintained homes, it's uncommon.

The Five Most Common Molds in Texas

1. **Alternaria** – A common outdoor mold often found on window frames, carpet, and textiles.
2. **Aspergillus** – Comes in many forms. Can be allergenic and may produce carcinogenic mycotoxins.
3. **Cladosporium** – Found outdoors but can move indoors. Known allergen; chronic exposure may lead to emphysema.
4. **Penicillium** – Found in soil, wallpaper, grains, and insulation. Difficult to identify but common.
5. **Stachybotrys** – The infamous "black mold." Dangerous but rare in well-kept homes.

Bonus: A Sixth Mold Worth Knowing

6. **Chaetomium** – Just as toxic as *Stachybotrys*. Found on paper and drywall. Known to cause:
   - Respiratory problems
   - Fatigue and joint pain
   - Nausea and migraines
   - Gastrointestinal distress

Both *Stachybotrys* and *Chaetomium* release mycotoxins that can mutate cells and contribute to diseases like cancer. They are classified as **"marker molds,"** meaning their presence is a strong indicator of a serious mold problem.

Toxic Mold Syndrome

Symptoms can affect the body physically, mentally, and emotionally. These include:

- Muscle aches
- Digestive issues
- Lymph node swelling
- Neurological problems
- Ringing in the ears
- Chronic fatigue

CHAPTER 7
COMMON MOLD INSPECTOR METHODS

There are three common mold testing methods used by professionals. Each inspector has their own preference, and each method is interpreted differently based on lab analysis. All are lab driven and left to the discretion of the inspector.

1. ERMI – Environmental Relative Moldiness Index
ERMI is a legitimate method—if you're a scientist studying indoor air quality. It collects **dust samples** from areas like door frames or behind appliances. Collecting dust will unsurprisingly result in a positive presence of spores. Essentially, no home will ever pass an ERMI test.

2. Swiffer
Swiffer suggests collecting samples from door jams, above the refrigerator, and other tucked away corners. Once Swiffer samples are mailed to their lab, the DNA is tested to identify mold spores within the dust. Swiffer generates a report of 36 common molds, identifying which are present on the subject property.

3. Air-O-Cell- Spore Trap Testing- This is the most widely used method in the industry and the one this book focuses on.
Air-O-Cell is an air sampling device collecting air samples in a cassette. This is designed for the rapid collection and analysis of a wide range of airborne aerosols. These include fungal spores, pollen, insect parts, skin fragments, fibers, and inorganic particulates. Air enters the cassettes, the particulates become impacted on the sampling substrate, and the air leaves through the exit orifice. The airflow and patented cassette housing is designed in such a way that particulates are distributed and deposited equally on a special glass slide contained in the cassette housing called the "trace."

Basically;

- A vacuum pump pulling air through a cassette.
- Mold spores impact a glass slide inside the cassette.
- A lab examines the slide under a microscope to identify and count spores.

Advantages of air sampling

1. If the fungal growth is not visible.
2. Quick and simple procedure. 1-5 minutes.
3. Fast turn-around times for quick results.
4. Low risk of cross-contamination.

Swab or Tape Sample Testing

Swab and tape tests are exactly what they sound like:

- **Swab Test:** A moistened cotton swab collects samples from a suspect surface.
- **Tape Lift:** A piece of clear tape presses against the surface and is placed on a microscope slide.

Both are sent to a lab to identify mold species present on visible surfaces.

Other Methods

- **Bulk Testing:** A piece of contaminated material (like drywall) is sent to a lab.
- **DIY Test Kits:** Often use petri dishes to grow mold. While they will always show something (mold is everywhere), they don't offer detailed insights and often cause more confusion than clarity.

In summary, while all testing methods have their place, **Air-O-Cell spore trap testing** is the industry standard for assessing airborne mold health. It's quick, efficient, and reliable—especially when done by a qualified inspector.

CHAPTER 8

UNDERSTANDING THE AIR-O-CELL MOLD LAB REPORT

When conducting an air sampling test, the first sample is taken **outside**—typically about ten feet from the front door. This provides a **baseline** for comparing indoor air quality.

The only time this sample is not done is during **inclement weather**—like rain, snow, or heavy winds—which can skew outdoor readings.

Why the Outdoor Sample Matters

In a healthy home, **indoor spore counts should be lower** than what's found outdoors. If the indoor air contains more spores than the baseline, it's a red flag for moisture problems, leaks, or hidden mold.

How to Read the Report

Lab reports usually contain three tested indoor areas per page. Each area includes three key columns:

The first (far left) column lists strains of mold A-Z.

The rest of the report is divided into three columns. Each represents a tested area. Each of those columns are divided into three sections.

The top line lists the area tested; example: outside, kitchen, bedroom, etc.

In each of the tested-area columns:

1. **Raw Spore Count** – The actual number of spores captured during sampling.
2. **Concentration (spores/m^3)** – This translates the raw number into a concentration per cubic meter of air. A reading under **500 spores/m^3** is typically considered normal.
3. **Percentage (%)** – The percentage that each strain of mold contributes to the total spore count.

Understanding the Air-O-Cell Mold Lab Report

Important Notes:

- **Sample Timing:** Most samples run for **five minutes**, pulling in 75 liters of air per minute. In dusty or dirty environments, a shorter 1-minute test may be used.
- **Grouped Mold Types:** Aspergillus and Penicillium are grouped together in reports because their spores are visually indistinguishable under the microscope.

Additional Report Sections

Mold lab reports are accompanied by two critical documents:

1. Assessment Report

Outlines:

- Property details
- Inspector credentials
- Purpose of the inspection
- Observations from each room (e.g., water damage, visible growth, odors)

It also includes a disclaimer: **no mold inspection can guarantee a mold-free home.** Mold can be hidden or return due to future moisture problems.

2. General Observations

Room-by-room notes include:

- Presence of visible growth
- Water damage or elevated moisture
- Recommendations for remediation (if needed)

Photos often accompany the report, showing:

- Air sample locations
- Moisture readings
- Suspected mold areas
- Air vents or questionable spaces

Spore Trap Report

Hygienitech Solutions
3131 West Loop S #417
Houston, TX, 77027
713-298-1449

Date Sampled: 06/11/2025
Date Received: 06/11/2025
Date Analyzed: 06/11/2025
Date Reported: 06/11/2025
Date Revised:
Project Name: ▓▓▓
Project Number: ▓▓▓
Project Address: ▓▓▓
Project City, State, ZIP: Houston, TX 77051

TEST METHOD: DIRECT MICROSCOPY EXAMINATION SEEML SOP 7   SEEML Reference #: H-250611089

Client Sample ID	3197			9741			3171		
Location	Outside			Kitchen			Master Bathroom		
Lab Sample ID	H-250611089-997			H-250611089-998			H-250611089-999		
Detection Limit (spores/m^3)	13			13			13		
Hyphal Fragments	2	27							
Pollen									
Spore Trap Used	AOC			AOC			AOC		
	raw ct.	spores/m^3	%	raw ct.	spores/m^3	%	raw ct.	spores/m^3	%
Alternaria (=Ulocladium)							1	13	1
Ascospores	64	853	4	40	533	14	20	267	10
Basidiospores	1400	18667	89	184	2453	63	92	1227	47
Bipolaris/Drechslera									
Cercospora									
Chaetomium									
Cladosporium	12	160	1	12	160	4	12	160	6
Colorless/Other Brown*									
Curvularia							1	13	1
Epicoccum									
Fusarium									
Memnoniella									
Nigrospora									
Oidium									
Penicillium/Aspergillus	92	1227	6	56	747	19	68	907	35
Pithomyces									
Polythrincium									
Pyricularia									
Rusts									
Smuts/Periconia/Myxomy							2	27	1
Spegazzinia									
Stachybotrys									
Tetraploa									
Torula									
Zygomycetes									
Background debris (1-5)**	3			3			3		
Sample Volume(liters)	75			75			75		
TOTAL SPORES/M^3	1568	20900		292	3890		196	2610	

Comments:
Spore types listed without a count or data entry were not detected during the course of the analysis for the respective sample, indicating a raw count of <1 spore.
The analytical sensitivity is the spores/m^3 divided by the raw count, expressed in spores/m^3. The limit of detection is the analytical sensitivity (in spores/m^3) multiplied by the sample volume (in liters) divided by 1000 liters.
*Colorless, other Brown are spores without a distinctive morphology on spore traps and non-viable surface samples.
**Background debris is the amount of particulate matter present on the slide and is graded from 1-5 with 1 = very light, 2= Light, 3 = Medium, 4 = Heavy, 5 = Very Heavy. The higher the rating the more likelihood spores may be underestimated. A rating of 5 should be interpreted as minimal counts and may actually be higher than reported.
***Ulocladium has been recognized by the International Mycological Association to be equal to Alternaria and so they are reported as one.
Disclaimer: The sample results are determined by the sample volume, which is provided by the customer.
This report relates only to the samples tested as they were received.
Respectfully submitted, SEEML

410 W Grand Pkwy S, Suite 250
Katy, TX. 77494
Phone: 832-437-2667

Magzoub Ismail
Magzoub Ismail, Approved Laboratory Signatory

AIHA LAP, LLC EMLAP #232339   Texas Lic: LAB1016
Form 18.0 Rev 5 01/21/22

CHAPTER 9

REMEDIATION, RESTORATION, TREATMENT

In Texas, if a home has **less than 25 contiguous square feet** of mold and minimal "marker" mold spores, treatment—not full remediation—is sufficient. In fact, nearly **90% of moldy homes** only need treatment. Some may require minor drywall removal, but not complete restoration.

However, treatment is only successful if **moisture, humidity, and water issues are resolved** first.

Remediation & Restoration

In Texas, full remediation requires a protocol written by a Licensed Mold Assessment Consultant (MAC). A Mold Remediation Contractor (MRC) then carries out the work. **The process includes:**

- Identifying moisture problems
- Containment of affected areas
- Removing or cleaning mold-damaged materials
- Ensuring proper cleanup and drying
- Ensuring the protection of the occupants and workers
- Post-remediation testing and certification

- **Treatment**

    Destroys both **active and dormant spores**, restoring the home's indoor air quality to normal health. It involves fogging or surface applications that denature mold. This treatment is effective for homes not containing "marker" molds or restoration. Post-treatment testing ensures that the air is clean and safe.

Misconceptions from Inspectors

Some mold inspectors still follow outdated remediation protocols and reject modern treatment methods. Many provide generic, "one-size-fits-all" protocols without considering less invasive, cost-effective solutions. Most will disagree with me. My take? They can write their own book. This book offers updated, real-world guidance.

Important Note

All homes have mold. No process—remediation, restoration, or treatment—can eliminate 100% of it. Mold spores exist **indoors and outdoors**. The goal is to control mold by managing humidity and moisture.

Before Any Work Begins, Ask These Questions:

- What is the exact problem and its cause?
- What's the scope of the work?
- What chemicals will be used?
- Will any belongings need to be removed or destroyed?
- How much of the home will be affected?
- Who will handle repairs?
- Will there be post-treatment testing?
- How long will the home need to be vacated?

CHAPTER 10
INTENTIONALLY OR UNINTENTIONALLY FAILED?

A mold inspector's responsibility is to determine the health of a home and have an accredited laboratory analyze collected samples. The professionally licensed mold inspector then provides an interpretational summary to the homeowner.

But not all inspectors interpret mold the same way. Over the years, I've reviewed numerous reports where inspectors recommended **extensive remediation**—even when no toxic molds or high spore counts were found, and the occupants had no classic symptoms.

Was it a difference in philosophy? Or just covering their assets?
Homes contain both live-able (breath-able) and non-live-able (non-breathable) areas.

Livable vs. Non-Livable Areas

There is a key distinction in mold testing:

- **Livable Areas:** Common areas: living rooms, bedrooms, family rooms, etc.
- **Non-Livable Areas:** Inner-walls, attics, under sinks, non-ventilated areas.

    Anything listed as "suspicious" fall under the discretion of the inspector.

There are areas of a home that will always test higher for mold spores:

- Ingress/egress points. Rooms close to the front and back door.
- Areas in close proximity to an attic access door that isn't well-sealed.
- Kitchens and bathrooms. (several water sources)

Important: Not all elevated spore counts in livable areas indicate a serious problem.

Non-livable Testing

Inner-wall (non-livable/breathable) areas are legitimate places to test. Especially on new construction. As mentioned earlier, builders are building for expedience. Closing a framed home after a heavy rain is a recipe for disaster.

- Wall testing (multiple-story home) to determine if an air-duct is producing moisture.
- Checking a plumbing pipe leak.

A plumbing leak can be easily detected with an infrared camera or moisture reader with pin points.

Those are legitimate testing areas that should be coupled with livable/breathable tested areas as well.

Repeating the following rule; *You either see it, smell it, or feel it* should determine how many air samples are taken.

Mold is facilitated by ambient moisture. Without adequate moisture, mold cannot grow or reproduce, but the spores do not die. They hibernate. Their survival mechanism allows mold to persist in fluctuating environments.

Dry mold is temporarily inactive. However, they are very light and can become airborne quite easily. This can quickly lead to spreading and the contamination of other areas.

Inner-wall mold testing will mostly reveal dormant mold. An inspector who disrupts the mold by banging on the wall is intentionally disturbing the mold. Disturbed mold sporulates, thus achieving the inspector's goal of intentional high "raw" spore counts.

Any inspector performing a drum solo on a wall should be immediately fired!

Is a home with inner-wall mold healthy?
Of course not, however 100% of homes in any humid region will test unhealthy.

Should a home receive major restoration to remove inner wall mold?
There are a lot of intangibles involved to provide a conclusive answer.

My personal opinion, I want to see air sampling completed in the living area of the home. Last time I checked, most home owners do not sniff inner-wall air.

If the inner-wall is opened, there is absolutely a need for treatment. Especially if there is a water breach.

Before spending thousands of dollars, hire an indoor environmental expert to test the health of the air. Do not rely solely on one mold inspector's conclusion.

Lastly, if a mold inspector informs you that your home is in need of major mold restoration, seek a physical examination.

Testing the inhabitants of the home for mold toxicity involves a combination of blood and urine tests. Blood testing measures antibodies produced in response to mold, while urine and stool testing can detect mold metabolites.

Again, seek a 2nd opinion!

Important note: Many mold inspectors are unfamiliar with the remediation process. They attach to the lab report an extensive (generic) mold-removal protocol. I typically toss it. One size does not fit all.

CHAPTER 11

DO-IT-YOURSELF COMMON MISTAKES

A general contractor can tear out drywall just like a mold mediator—but that doesn't mean they should. They may unknowingly spread mold spores, turning a small issue into a much bigger one.

As the legendary oil firefighter Red Adair once said: **"If you think it's expensive to hire a professional, wait until you hire an amateur."**

Common DIY Mold Mistakes

1. **Not knowing what to keep vs. what to discard**
   Some items can be cleaned and saved. Others must go. Knowing the difference is critical.

2. **Using ineffective cleaning solutions**
   Bleach? Vinegar? Baking soda? Not all solutions work on all materials.

3. **Lack of proper containment**
   Without containment barriers, spores spread easily to clean areas. This mistake is one of the costliest.

4. **Ignoring the HVAC system**
   Mold in air ducts or returns can be blown throughout the home. Always clean or treat the HVAC system as part of remediation.

5. **Inadequate protective gear**
   Mold spores can enter through the nose, mouth, eyes, ears—even open skin. Without sealed goggles, respirators, gloves, and suits, you're putting yourself at risk.

6. **Incorrect use of protective gear**
   Wearing gear is one thing. Fitting it properly is another. Even the best equipment won't help if it's used wrong.

DIY can work—for small surface mold on hard materials. But for anything more, especially involving porous surfaces or suspected mycotoxins, **call a professional**.

CHAPTER 12
PREP FOR SELLING

According to Realtor.com, here are their 12 tips for selling your home:

1. Find a great agent
2. Improve curb appeal
3. Declutter living areas
4. Depersonalize your space
5. Repaint walls in neutral colors
6. Touch up scuffs and marks
7. Fix loose handles
8. Add plants
9. Conduct a smell test
10. Clean, clean, clean
11. Hide valuables
12. Consider staging

Those are solid suggestions, but let me offer you a **mold-focused checklist**—one that could save your deal:

Ed's Mold-Smart Checklist

- **Look up.** Seriously. Look at the ceilings in every room.
- **Check closets.** Especially corners and ceilings.
- **Check under every sink.** Any signs of leaks or water stains?
- **Air vents and filters.** Replace air filters and inspect for dust or discoloration.
- **Paint over old water stains.** Even if the issue was fixed 20 years ago, buyers and inspectors will still ask about it.
- **Clean out closets and pantries.** Dormant mold hides in dark, unventilated areas.
- **Duct cleaning.** Hire a pro to clean ducts, coils, vents, and the HVAC plenum.
- **Avoid mold traps.** Don't leave wet coats or sweaty shoes in enclosed spaces.

Prevention Is Peace of Mind

Mold spores are everywhere. They'll find comfort in any undisturbed, humid area. But this doesn't always mean you need remediation. **90% of mold concerns can be resolved with treatment.**

Be Proactive—Not Reactive

A limited pre-listing mold inspection (with air testing and visual checks) can prevent unwanted surprises. Home inspectors appreciate working with mold pros. Many will even consult with us before finalizing their report.

With a little preparation and the right knowledge, you can **protect your sale, your home's value, and your peace of mind**.

CHAPTER 13

WATER DOESN'T CAUSE MOLD

One of my social media posts stirred up quite the storm in the mold industry. I said, *"Water intrusion doesn't cause mold."*

Technically, that's not wrong—it's just not what most people are used to hearing.

Water, humidity, and moisture don't **cause** mold. They **activate** it. Mold is already present—everywhere. Water simply allows it to colonize.

If a water issue is dried within 48 hours, **mold shouldn't become a problem**. But leave it longer, and mold takes over. So yes, water is the *trigger*, but **not the root cause**.

On "Mold Experts"

The more I study mold, the more I realize—**there are no true mold experts.** There are a lot of self-proclaimed ones, but give them enough time to talk, and you'll notice how they believe their own bullshit.

I don't consider myself an expert. I'm a **student of mold**. The deeper I dig, the more questions I find.

Slime Mold Fascination

I'm currently deep into a book about *Myxomycetes*—slime molds. They have characteristics of both **fungi and animals**. It's like reading a sci-fi novel… only it's real.

Bottom line: Water does not cause mold. It simply **wakes up** what's already waiting.

CHAPTER 14
SAFE HOME REMEDIES

There are several natural, at-home options that can help reduce or eliminate mold in small, manageable areas. While these solutions are **not replacements for professional remediation**, they can be useful tools in your mold-fighting arsenal.

Essential Oils

Based on studies published in the *International Journal of Occupational and Environmental Health* and *Reviews on Environmental Health*, the following essential oils have mold-fighting properties:

- **Clove Oil**
- **Tea Tree Oil**
- **Eucalyptus Oil**
- **Lavender Oil**
- **Citrus Oil**
- **Grapefruit Seed Extract**

These oils can be diluted and applied to non-porous surfaces or used in diffusers to improve air quality.

Other Household Solutions

- **Vinegar:** Spray undiluted white vinegar on moldy areas. Let it sit, scrub, and rinse.
- **Baking Soda:** Often used in tandem with vinegar to tackle different types of mold.
- **Hydrogen Peroxide:** Effective on light mold growth— spray and scrub as needed.
- **Chlorine Dioxide:** A powerful treatment option via fogging or spray. Use with caution and proper ventilation.

Important Warning

NEVER mix bleach with ammonia.
   The combination is **deadly**—literally.

Know When to Call a Pro

These remedies can help with surface mold or serve as a preventive measure. But if the issue is structural, recurring, or linked to moisture problems, **call a licensed mold professional**.

CHAPTER 15
HORSES & MOLD

In the 1920's, in Ukraine, horses began getting sick from a mysterious disease.

It wasn't until two decades later, after thousands of horses had died across Ukraine and Russia, that Russian scientists identified the culprit. The horses had been eating moldy hay.

In the 1940's, the deadly fungus got its name; Stachybotrys. It wasn't until 30 years later that the associated toxin was identified.

It wasn't until 1970 that we knew that toxin was coming from Stachybotrys. Also, in the early 1900's, thousands of people died of the disease caused by mold food/grains.

In 1977, there was an outbreak of Stachybotryotoxicosis among farm workers handling infested straw in Hungry.

In 1996, workers at a horticultural facility in Germany developed very painful, inflamed lesions on their fingers followed by scaling of the skin when they handled decomposable pots infested with S. chartarum.

CHAPTER 16
GLUTEN ALLERGIES

Mold toxicity is becoming a more common problem for those struggling with mysterious chronic degenerative disease. Many people convert to gluten-free and immediately feel better. And then, start feeling worse. If this has been your experience with the gluten free diet, you might want to investigate mold and mold toxins. *Why?* Mold and gluten can cause a lot of the same types of symptoms.

Before diving into the symptoms of mold toxicity, it is important to point out a few things for clarity. Yeast (sometimes referred to as Candida) is a type of mold that can inhabit the sinus cavities, the mouth, the GI tract, the lungs, skin, and other tissues of the body. An overgrowth of this type of yeast has been linked to human disease. That being said, there are other species of mold that can grow on and in humans that also contribute to disease.

There are also forms of environmental molds that can grow on foods and in the home. These molds can produce toxin byproducts often times referred to as mycotoxins. Mycotoxins have been linked to a number of health conditions to include immune suppression and cancer.

When thinking about mold toxicity, keep in mind that some people are allergic to mold, some have internal mold (yeast) infections that create symptoms, some have high levels of mold growing in their homes, and some people react to the mycotoxins...sometimes all four. So, for clarity's sake, the symptoms of mold toxicity can be related to all four.

https://www.glutenfreesociety.org

CHAPTER 17
MOLD IN THE BIBLE

Yes, mold is mentioned in the Bible. I believe the first mention was when Eve told Adam not to eat the fuzzy plum and to grab a shiny ripe apple instead.

I could be mistaken, but for the sake of writer's license, let's just go with that.

The Bible speaks on the subject of mold in **Leviticus 14:33 - 48**. The original word translated "mildew" or "mold" in this passage is literally the word for "leprosy." God wanted His people to live in a mold-free environment, showing his concern for their well-being.

We know today that the presence of mold or mildew in a house contributes to allergies, asthma, bronchitis, and other breathing difficulties.

The Mosaic Law commanded the Israelites to remove mildew from their houses and gave step-by-step instructions on how to do it. The Lord had them take preventative measures to protect their health. Then as now, getting rid of mold was important.

Did God own the first ServPro franchise?

CHAPTER 18
I NEED A MOLD INSPECTION

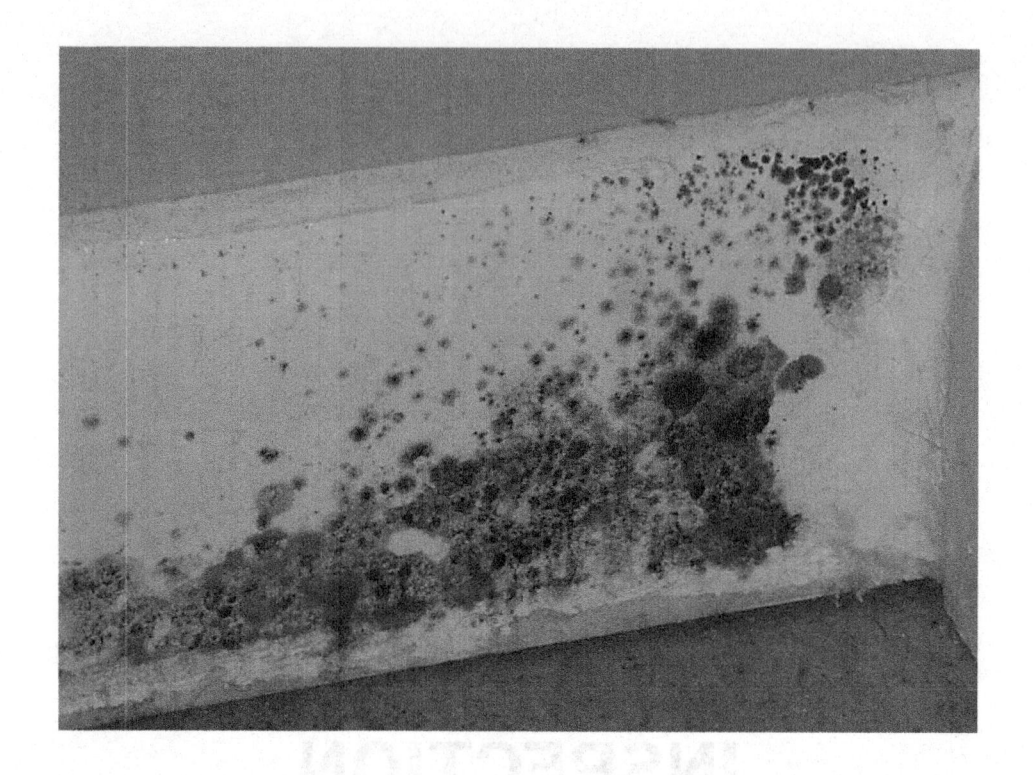

Many times, a conversation will begin, *"I need a mold inspection."*

"Do you see it, smell it, or feel?" I ask. *"I see it, do you want me to send a picture?"* The above picture is an example of such conversation.

The homeowner needed a treatment, not an inspection. Sure, I could have charged for an inspection and returned later to provide treatment, however I provide free testing post-treatment to ensure the home is healthy. So, we saved the homeowner an additional fee.

Amusingly, many times when I've conveyed to a homeowner (after lab testing) their home was healthy, I detected a little disappointment in their tone.

CHAPTER 19

10 MOST COMMON MOLD MYTHS

#1. Mold can be totally eliminated from a home.

Virtually impossible.

#2. Bleach kills mold.

Only on non-porous objects. It discolors, not kills.

#3. If you don't see it, it doesn't exist.

Mold is ubiquitous.

#4. Dead mold can't make you sick.

Denatured mold can't make you sick. Dead mold should be treated as living mold.

#5. All black mold is deadly.

The color of mold is based on its food source.

#6. Mold testing is critical to determining if a home has mold.

Mold does three things; grows, sporulates, or sits dormant. Air sampling can be misleading.

#7. No odor, no mold.

Not all molds have odors.

#8. Mold has no benefits.

Our ecosystem relies on mold.

#9. You should not worry about a small spot of mold.

Size is not an indication of a problem, but it could trigger an issue.

#10. Your family physician will know how to treat mold toxicity.

Some doctors are healers, some are drug dealers. Seek a specialist.

CHAPTER 20
PURCHASING A RESALE

No one knows a home better than the people who've lived in it. But most homeowners know very little about mold—and even less about its history inside their own walls.

If you're purchasing a resale home, these are the **critical questions** you should be asking (even if the seller can't answer all of them):

Water and Mold History Checklist

- Has there ever been a **sewer backup**?
- Have **sinks** or **toilets** ever leaked?
- Has the **dishwasher** ever overflowed?
- Has the **refrigerator** or **ice maker** ever leaked?
- Has the **washing machine** ever leaked, backed up, or overflowed?
- Has there ever been a **burst pipe**—anywhere in the house?
- Has **groundwater** ever entered the home from outside?
- Has any **shower** unit or **tile** been replaced?

If the seller doesn't know—or refuses to answer—**don't panic**, but do take action. This is when a **qualified mold inspector** becomes essential.

You're not just buying a home. You're buying its **history**—and in some cases, its hidden health hazards.

CHAPTER 21
TEXAS DEPARTMENT OF LICENSING AND REGULATION

As mentioned earlier, FEMA classifies mold as a **natural disaster**. Here is the surprising part: unlike asbestos removal, **mold remediation is not standardized across the United States**. Some states have adopted guidelines or passed legislation to regulate microbial containment and removal, but many have not.

Fortunately, **Texas is a license-required state** for both mold inspectors and remediators. If you live in Texas, you can verify credentials directly through the Texas Department of Licensing and Regulation (TDLR).

Sadly, there are still con artists in this industry. If a remediator guarantees a "mold-free" home—**run**. No home is, or ever will be, mold-free.

Many inspectors, like some physicians, resist continuing education or fail to update their practices. **Use your instincts.** Make sure any inspector or remediator you work with is **properly licensed and insured**.

And remember: the TDLR website is also the place to **file a complaint** if you suspect misconduct by a licensed (or unlicensed) mold professional.

CHAPTER 22
REAL LIFE STORIES

Amanda's Story

Growing up, mold was never something my parents warned me about—and society doesn't exactly teach us to worry about it either. I assumed that if mold were an issue, I'd have obvious signs like sneezing or congestion.

In 2023, I rented a house that checked all the boxes: a safe neighborhood, a great location, and a nice backyard for my boys to play in. I knew the area had flooded during Hurricane Harvey, but the landlord had remodeled—new kitchen, bathrooms, and updated flooring. For a home built in 1948, it looked great.

But gradually, things started to feel... off.

I lost motivation to go outside. Brain fog became a daily struggle. My older son was always congested. My younger son had constant nosebleeds. There was no bathroom ventilation—where was all the shower steam going? Then I noticed water stains on the ceiling. The landlord claimed it was just a minor AC issue. A handyman came out, painted over the stains, and reassured me it wasn't mold.

Still, I had doubts. A friend encouraged me to do an **ERMI test**. The results showed extremely high levels of **Aspergillus** and **Penicillium**—both tied to water-damaged buildings.

I showed the results to my landlord. He refused to let me out of the lease, accusing me of fabricating the issue to break the contract.

Then came the health tests. My kids and I all tested extremely high for **Ochratoxin**, a mycotoxin produced by those same mold strains. Eventually, we were all diagnosed with **Chronic Inflammatory Response Syndrome (CIRS)**. I also developed **optic neuritis**, which left me with limited vision in my right eye.

The past year has been a life-altering journey of detoxing, healing, and advocating—for myself and my kids.

Allison's Story

The Road to Recovery

My son and I experienced mystery symptoms for months—eczema, asthma, neurological problems, and chronic fatigue. We visited several specialists and kept getting worse until we finally discovered **mold** as the root cause.

Mold illness—also known as **Chronic Inflammatory Response Syndrome (CIRS)**—can leave toxins called **mycotoxins** in the body for long periods, especially in those who are sensitive.

Symptoms vary based on genetics and exposure. Some children may even develop **Pediatric Acute-Onset Neuropsychiatric Syndrome (PANS)** with symptoms like behavioral changes or sudden OCD.

Common symptoms include:

- Sinus congestion
- Sleep disturbances
- Joint pain
- Itchy, watery eyes
- Wheezing or asthma
- Brain fog and exhaustion
- Food intolerances and digestive issues
- Anxiety and bloating

Steps to Healing

Before detoxing from mold, you must first lay a strong foundation:

- **Hydration**: Drink half your body weight in ounces of filtered water daily.
- **Nutrition**: Eat a variety of fruits, vegetables, lean meats, fish, and healthy fats.
- **Sunlight**: Aim for 15 minutes of morning sun daily.
- **Sleep**: Get at least 8 hours each night for optimal repair.

- **Digestion**: Daily bowel movements are essential to remove mycotoxins. Magnesium citrate can help regulate elimination.

Support the **liver, kidneys, and lymphatic system** with:

- **Binders** like zeolite, charcoal, or carbon-based supplements
- **Gentle detox methods**: walking, sauna sessions, deep breathing
- **Natural anti-inflammatories**: omega-3s and turmeric

Gut and Mitochondrial Repair

Mold often leads to:

- **Candida overgrowth**
- **Leaky gut**
- **Food sensitivities**

Eliminate:

- Dairy
- Sugar
- Alcohol
- Gluten

Add:

- Probiotics
- Herbal or homeopathic remedies for candida
- COQ10 and methylated B vitamins to support mitochondria

Histamine and Mold

Mold raises **histamine** levels in the body—think of it like an overflowing bucket. While healing, avoid **high-histamine** and **high-mold** foods like:

- Chocolate
- Peanuts & peanut butter
- Dried fruits
- Fermented foods (sauerkraut, pickles)
- Aged cheeses
- Beer, wine, cider
- Spinach, tomatoes, mushrooms, avocados
- Processed meats
- Soy sauce
- Yogurt and kefir

DAO enzyme supplements can help reduce histamine load during meals.

Thanks to **Naturopathy and mold remediation**, we've healed. I even returned to school to become a **Traditional Naturopath**. Now, I help others recover from mold illness and other chronic conditions that traditional medicine often overlooks.

www.heightsofhealth.com

THE FINAL CHAPTER

Remediator? I hardly know her.

I know, mold is nothing to laugh about. If this book contains one valuable lesson: Pay attention to your health.

That nagging cough.

Regular migrains.

Sudden nose bleeds.

Chronic respiratory issues.

Most importantly:

Do you feel better out of your home than in your home?

Do you feel better out of your workplace than in your workplace?

When one person suffers unusual symptoms in a household, we refer to them as *"the canary in the coal mine."* They are breathing the same air as you, your health is no less affected.

This book is a source to understand the basics of mold. Be your own health advocate. Seek professional medical advice. Trust your instincts and be healthy!

Thank you!

Ed Kampf

TESTIMONIALS

"Ed's service is amazing!"
My kids were constantly sick, and our medical practitioner suggested mold testing. The lab results showed toxic mold in every room of our house. Ed came out immediately and treated our home. The follow-up lab report showed **ZERO mold spores**—his process got everything!

I also had him treat our new construction home for off-gassing fumes. The results were incredible. My son, who used to cough all night, hasn't coughed since. I have more energy and far less brain fog.

— *Grateful Parent*

"As a fellow mold inspector, I trust Ed."
Edward is professional, knowledgeable, and effective. I've personally seen his product eliminate mold spore counts in homes. I confidently recommend him to anyone dealing with mold or allergy concerns.

— *Licensed Mold Inspector*

"Honest, thorough, and reassuring."
After a mold scare, I called Ed to inspect our home. He was upfront, answered all my questions, and conducted air sampling. It turns out our home was just fine—and Ed gave us peace of mind. Thank you, Ed!

— *Homeowner*

"Ed gave us peace of mind before buying our new home."
We had an outstanding experience with Hygienitech Solutions, LLC, and Mr. Ed Kampf. He accommodated us on short notice and performed a thorough inspection. He was professional, kind, and incredibly knowledgeable.

Not only did he inspect the home, but he also educated us on mold prevention. His **same-day report** gave us the confidence to move forward, knowing our new home was safe for our family.

— *Future Homeowners*

"SAME-DAY results and peace of mind before listing my home."

My realtor recommended Ed to make sure there were no unseen mold issues before listing. Ed came out the **very next day**, and I had results **that same evening**.

He explained everything clearly—from common molds to the more harmful types—and reassured me the air in my home was healthy. I was able to move forward with peace of mind. I highly recommend Ed for his expertise and kindness.

— Seller Preparing to List

"High-quality service at a fraction of the cost."
We discovered mold behind the refrigerator due to a leaking valve. After replacing the drywall, Ed came out within days to perform a treatment.

He provided a detailed lab report, and the best part—**his pricing was a fraction of what other companies charge**. Great experience, professional service, and trustworthy results.

— Satisfied Client

BIO

Edward Kampf's journey of selling;
From Orange Juice (Minute Maid) to Wine...
From Wine to Cognac (Remy Martin). ...
From Cognac to Mortgage.. ..
From Mortgages to Mold...
which birthed; **From Mold to Sold**.

Edward's first book, **"Your Home is Mamng You Sick"** *How to Create a Healthy Home* can be purchased on Amazon.

His one-how CE class, **"Understanding Mold"** is rated as one of the best CE classes by many of the top Realtors in the Greater Houston Area.

Hygienitech Solutions, LLC. is a disnptor in the mold testing/remediation industry, providing affordable, honest assessment and solutions in an industry saturated with profiters.

Edward Kampf
TDLR #MAC2019
www.hygienitechsolutions.com
ed@hygienitechsolutions.com
713-298-1449

SPECIAL THANKS

Heather Cox- CoxRoxCo (cover design)
Mold Matters Podcasts
Amanda Vlastas
Allison McHorter
Darren M. Palmer — www.selfpublishn30days.com

Rick Figueroa
Chair

Thomas F. Butler
Vice Chair

Gerald R. Callas, M.D., F.A.S.A.
Nora Castañeda
Sujeeth Draksharam
Lori High, R.N., N.P., Retired
Gary F. Wesson, D.D.S., M.S.

Mold Assessment Consultant
EDWARD KAMPF

License Number: MAC2019

The person named above is licensed by the Texas Department of Licensing and Regulation.

License Expires: February 07, 2026

Brian E. Francis
Interim Executive Director

HYGIENITECH SOLUTIONS

MOLD TESTING
ODOR & MOLD REMOVAL

MOLD & MILDEW

Breathe Easy with Our Services

- Honest mold inspection evaluations
- Creating healthy homes
- Environmentally safe solutions
- Air Duct Protectant -12 month Mold-free

FREE REALTOR CE

- Staying Healthy in an Unhealthy Environment #45039 | 2 Hours
- Understanding Mold #49209 | 1 Hour

TEST RESULTS WITHIN 24 HOURS

Call For Free Estimates

713.298.1449

Testimonials
★★★★★

Ed and his services are unlike anything I have seen. Thanks, Ed for making my client's home safe prior to move in day!

Ed's treatment helped salvage my real estate deal with buyers hyper concerned about air quality due to having a young child. He is knowledgeable, easy to work with and very practical in his approach! I would definitely recommend his services!

My son used to cough all night long. Since Ed's treatment, his cough has resolved! I've also noticed I have a lot more energy and less brain fog.

hygienitechsolutions.com
ed@hygienitechsolutions.com

Licensed Mold Assessment Consultant — TDLR #MAC2019

HYGIENITECH SOLUTIONS

UNDERSTANDING MOLD

Complimentary 1 Hour CE
Course #49209

RealStar-U, LLC TREC Provider 10296

This course is designed exclusively for real estate agents seeking to expand their knowledge on mold-related issues in real estate transactions.

WHAT YOU WILL LEARN:

- **How to Read a Mold Inspection:**
    - Decode and understand mold inspection reports effectively.
- **Identifying Intentional Failures:**
    - Learn why and how some mold inspectors may intentionally fail homes and how to spot these red flags.
- **Remediation vs. Quick Fixes:**
    - Understand the differences between proper remediation and quick, ineffective fixes.
- **Common Strains of Mold:**
    - Familiarize yourself with the most common strains of mold found in homes.
- **Mold Prevention Tips:**
    - Discover effective strategies to prevent mold growth and protect your property.

Call to Schedule Class
713.298.1449

yourhomeismakingyousick.com

TESTIMONIALS
★★★★★

Much needed course!

This needs to be a mandatory class!

Very educational.

This information was extremely helpful.

Ed Kampf | Licensed Mold Assessment Consultant
TDLR #MAC2019

hygienitechsolutions.com
ed@hygienitechsolutions.com

This book is from the perspective of a professionally licensed Mold Assessment Consultant.

In Texas, a Mold Assessment Consultant (MAC) is a state-licensed professional who assesses mold issues and writes mold remediation protocols. They are required to have specific training and pass an exam administered by the Texas Department of Licensing and Regulation (TDLR). MACs are responsible for identifying the cause of mold, determining the extent of damage, and creating a plan for remediation.

FEMA classifies mold in the same breath as other natural disasters; *fires, floods, hurricanes, tornados, tsunamis, etc.*

In addition to health risks, mold can have a major effect on the value of a home. The largest single investment ever made can turn out to be largest financial mistake a homeowner can ever make.

But that shouldn't induce panic. Over 90% of residential mold issues require treatment, not restoration. Mold is ubiquitous. It's unavoidable, especially in humid areas of our country. Heck, mold even exists on the Space Station.

This book is a must read for all Homeowners, Realtors, Property Managers, Builders, Investors, Flippers, Contractors, Inspectors, Reuters, Buyers, Sellers, Allergists/Physicians.

Made in the USA
Monee, IL
29 August 2025